BLOOD WRITING

BLOOD WRITING

For Dear Sally
with
Fond admiration,

12/27/17

POEMS

SEAN SEXTON

Sean

ANHINGA PRESS

TALLAHASSEE, FLORIDA 2010

Cover art: "Lament for Lost Fruit," oil on canvas, 72" x 90", 2001-2003,
by the author
Cover design, book design, and production: Carol Lynne Knight
Typesetting: Jill Runyan
Type Styles: text set in Adobe Garamond Pro; titles set in Tieopolo;
ornament from P22 Victorian Ornaments 2

Library of Congress Cataloging-in-Publication Data
Blood Writing by Sean Sexton, First Edition
ISBN – 978-1-934695-19-7
Library of Congress Cataloging Card Number – 2010928796

This publication is sponsored in part by a grant
from the Florida Department of State,
Division of Cultural Affairs, and the Florida Arts Council.

Anhinga Press Inc. is a nonprofit corporation dedicated wholly to the publication and appreciation of fine poetry and other literary genres.

For personal orders, catalogs and information write to:
Anhinga Press
P.O. Box 3665
Tallahassee, Florida 32315
Website: www.anhinga.org
E-mail: info@anhinga.org

Published in the United States
by Anhinga Press
Tallahassee, Florida
First Edition, 2010

For Sharon

CONTENTS

ACKNOWLEDGMENTS

Grateful acknowledgment to publications and venues in which these poems first appeared, sometimes in a different form:

Florida Review: "The Dragmark" and "A Horse Dies Beneath You"

New Delta Review: "Chaos"

2008 Poetry Now Calendar: "Postholedigger's Dream"

Journal of the American Guild of Organists: "To the Organ"

Sections I, IV, and V of "To the Organ" were presented by Eliut Daniel Flores during the 2004 Organ Concert series at Community Church, Vero Beach, FL in a program entitled, "Who is the King of Instruments? An Organ and Piano Duel."

"Song of the South" was drafted and presented with the painting of the same title in the 1991 Annual Juried Exhibition at The Orlando Museum of Art, Orlando, FL.

BLOOD WRITING

FIELD WORK

TIME

No man is cheated of life who's lived through ten generations of cattle.

In my life, there
have always been cattle.
Year in, year out, their
hides a calendar written
with fire.

New heifers weaned this fall,
grown out and bred;
numbers branded on them
in late summer, peeling
as they calve.

The '60s heifers I saw born,
weaned, fed at the trough,
watched birth their calves.
all —
now gone.

The '70s, last of them sold in September,
toothless, raw-boned cows
marching up the loading ramp
into a truck to market,
leaving

pastures filled with great-grandaughters
fleshed and springing, keeping
a place in time within
boundaries of post
and wire.

Count your days among the cattle.
Man is the emperor of time.

FIELD WORK

for Wendell Berry
The favor of the king is like dew upon the grass.
— Prov. 19: 12

Morning.
The land is an open hand.
You enter the field of rising mist, drop
your blade into the tilth, and take off —
cutting its face and grain, turning it
upon itself, rending roots and rhizomes, grasp
of the previously entered: a coterie
of squatters, beggars, and importune
lives that hold no lease in this world
save that which we all hold.

In an hour appointed to spiders and worms,
you make your rounds, spewing smoke,
fume, and deafening sound, crossing ground
so wet, so new, you wonder if you
should be there at all. A wake of
halved, broken things left in your passing,
remembrance itself upended
as you go.

The orb climbs the sky — loosing a breeze, sending
shadows to the ends of the field.

By noon the field is in ruin, wave upon wave
of broken sod, a frozen sea of disturbance, market-
place of harmed things, arguing at full value
(profiteers gone with the mist). The white birds are making
no deal with anything save they consume all,
keeping at the edge of your progress, catching

everything that moves (one finds an injured
mouse it can't quite swallow).

A rabbit cowers lower each pass
closer between you and him
in the grass,
breaking all at once, racing
across the field, dodging overpassing
shadows in fear, rolling like a ball into its
pocket
on the far fence.

*The day in full glare; it's time to stop, rest, and repast as light
moves to the other side of the trees.*

A bright afternoon return, so bright out there,
you barely find your trace on the land.
The ground, clenched like a fist, the map of work
lost against blurred distances.
You try to know where you should be,
looking where you've been, to see
where you next go, doubling over or
running past along your way, searching,
wasting seed if you're planting,
fuel and time regardless,
wasting yourself upon this ground,
grinding against its substance,

driving,
thinking,
watching,
waiting,

as ever you are moving, circling
on a course, making patterns for a time,
and that time is called
your life.

The afternoon unfolds: ground begins opening like a night-blooming flower,
air takes on color.

Quickly now, things change,
quickness itself a change.
The western sky is emptying of birds heading east.
Other creatures appear as light is pouring
over the rim of the world.
Shadows
like fingers grow, taking the land
in their grasp, reaching the far edge
of the field as you reach the other.
In lightfall, beguiling brilliance.
Last moments belong to the worker,
before light, time,
and effort
empty
into
dark.

Distant trees barely perceptible against the lights of town,
stars emergent, sliver of moon.
Latch the gate by feel on the way out.

PALMS

Those tall, thin
pillars just reach
shaggy heads
they tie to
the ground.

Patterns
engrain
their
silver
hides,

every bulge
and
pedicle
of
a walk
heavenward
(only heaven knows
how long).

Imagine
life's
message
to thrive
and
be well
traversing
that length.

Seasons passed
bearing tumult,

drought, flood,
and freeze.

How they
eat, drink,
and respire,

take
mysterious
commands
of bloom
and regress,
the gain and
shedding of
fronds,

each moment
as if life is
an ongoing
ceremony of
appointments

kept in quiet,
unbroken
mortality,
standing
upon
our wisdom.

DITCH CLEANING

Darkness is born in the middle of the day.
— Zulu proverb

It brings up the past
(A steel dinosaur feeds in the distance, perched
on the ditchbank along the road).
This house of strain rolls full-scream
on tracks, swinging
boom-borne buckets through the air,
a grab at a time.

In a wake of muck and swill:
vegetation, ditchgrass, hyacinths,
small trees, and detritus, mud-
soaked logs, tires, bottles, and
other things from beneath the world
thrown on the bank in heaps,
in stark morning light.

And middlemen of the ditch,
everywhere, scattered
in the spoil,
emerging:

litter of fishes —

tilapia,
bream,
crappie,
mullet, and bass,
on the road in the same gasp, some

flipping, others supine, quiet,
or runover into flattened
fish-shapes.

A huge gar, choking in the air,
rolled and battered in dirt, frying in the sun,
others selling cheap in the bird-market,
as egrets,
storks,
and vultures
arrive to quarrel and bid.

Archaic mudfish and mud puppies,
pathetic dog-faced eels, somnambulant
from watery night, gathered into
soft circles of themselves, resigned
to their plight. Apple snails strewn
and shut tight, catfish set in their business of crawling
and indecipherable things, mauled or crushed
by the machine, unnamable as the never
before seen, large, black, winged waterborne insects.

Last, and in greatest number:
Crayfish, "Crawdads," lobsters in miniature,
hundreds in every sector,
set off on journeys down the road,
or holding ground, fighting gear ready
in defiance of everything. Semiloads of citrus blow by as they stand
like union soldiers at Chancellorsville, twenty
crushed in one passing, the rest,
angry and fearless, ready to fight,

keeping eye to eye with you
as you try to catch (claws rising on contact)
and hold them like set mousetraps to fling
ditchward; twenty thrown, twenty more
appear, crawling from the spoil
like some new creature
deigned to take over the world.
Next morning waiting for the school bus,
they're everywhere on the road: some at the ends of tiny trails

of footprints where they gave up and fell over,
running on legs that go
nowhere.
Others, flattened in tire tracks,
currency of a scheme
that spends them
grandly, indiscriminately
to buy some undivined thing
of the world.

Days pass.
Spoil shrinks, cures, and cracks,
becomes a bed for sprouting grass.
Stains hammer dry into fines
aflight in dust of passing traffic.
Scraps of carcass, leaf, and scale
drift and gather to the edge of the road,
subsume in its berm.

Months later,
fragments of wood,

shell, and bone
harden into the grain
and substance of the road
beside the ditch running
through the middle of our lives out to the ends
of the world

SPRING LIGHT

Like truth too strong
to know at once,
this early light of spring —
its harmful radiance, keeps
everything huddled in shade.

Worst is the shank of day
when the little leaf engines
in the grass run hardest, spinning,
until they're all
burned up,

and darkness shuts them down, sends
the world to bed. Mist rises in the field
afterward, from things overwrought,
thickening into fog
through the night.

Morning fruit of light
sheds its orange husk, gathers blue
bedding from the sky, climbing
shrinking into a hard core
of fire,

shedding light by which
rivers are halted,
oceans emptied,
ground ruined,
worlds destroyed.

The pasture's undoing
these days and weeks,
much of a season
until somehow
increasing —

thatch
fills the least-houred hollows,
longest kept shadows afield —
bringing each time
around

in long,
slow tides,
what must and shall come,
as belief with
understanding.

June.
Rains arrive,

lifting spirits, loosing fear,
filling udders, fleshing backs,
tongues and teeth working all the while
as they
come.

Ingestion,
elimination,
doors flinging wide
in the enterprise of being,
torrents of urine,

shit flowing
like batter into
cakes —
glistening like mirrors
in the morning light.

LAST DAYS

Among these last

disconsolate days of summer,

I lie on the daybed after lunch

gazing through window screen.

Light has gone over to

the other side of the trees,

white hot air outside

motionless as an insect's gaze.

The buzzing of cicadas

high in the yard

apprehends

the quiet.

Thunder soft in the distance,

makes its way,

unbidden solution

to the unendurable day.

SONG OF THE SOUTH

Salt the melon,
wound its sweetness with salt and eat!

Sow the bellies into the greens.
Like the cookstove pot, the soil is full
of forgotten things.

"Good and evil," say the Menorcans,
"are the same when they're past."

Raise a song,
let Southern voices sing —

We are indentured to this age,
to the past, to one another,
and the land unto us all.

Raise a song Southerners, sing!
To make one, many lives are needed.

BLOOD WRITING

IN THE PENS

This morning I return to retrieve
what we left in the dark.
Scattered around the table
and overbrimming trash barrel
at the center of the workplace,
tools and litter of our labors:
shovel, prybar, hammer, nail bucket and saw,
hotshots, sorting sticks, plastic worm-medicine containers
and dose syringe,
fly-dope reservoir and gun,
brown glass vaccine bottles — each with a remaining
thimbleful of fluid,
inside out, manured and bloody
obstetrical sleeves stuffed in cardboard boxes,
empty water bottles, used hypodermic needles,
syringes, and their plastic cases, cans of orange spray paint,
two half-empty canisters of blood-stopper
powder, and discarded surgical gloves.

Pairs of dehorners and noseleads are pulled
from the bucket of iodine as its contents are flung
to the trodden barrens of the
bottom lot.

All these things, imported into the hot,
Floridian workday, languish amid the ordinary
detritus of bent nails and broken boards of unusable
lengths
in set aside heaps.

The floor of the chute is clogged, its gate frozen
with mud, spatters of blood, manure and spills of worm medicine

decorate the head-catch and platform and horns
in all colors and sizes litter the dirt out front.

These and the patterned ground remain —

as though some great event took place,
parade or public gathering, cast among many lives, spread
to every sector and space of the bowing,
weathered walls of the pens.

A wave of guilt passes through me ...

We were in such a rush,
the heat of the day upon us
as we brought them in, divided
the herd, pushing cows into the crevice,
parting calves, a crowding-pen load at a time,
down the wooden runway filled end to end
with them as we worked
a head
at a time.

The banging hips, slamming gates,
stinging needles, slicing blades,
irons burning, and electric prods,
all applied to them as they funneled
through our hands,
injected,
dewormed,
dehorned, altered,
ear-tagged, paint-numbered,
checked on a list, and
let go.

The stream of them,
fluid at times, till they
halted with incidence, crammed into knots
the crew had to undo.
One calf on his back, wedged
from trying to turn around.
We ran others past
till the chute emptied
and he could be straightened,
gotten on his feet, caught
and worked
and the flow resumed.

"Be careful, they're hot!"
I shouted above the roaring brand heater
"We might lose one if we're not careful."
Like the large steer that balked
at the entrance to the squeeze — turning around
each time and pushing past, calf by calf
to the back, till none were left.
We caught him as the cows started in,
the first of them chocking his retreat, forcing him
to the head-catch where he stood,
eyes blinking,
tongue lathering.

We stopped to cool him
like a fighter between rounds,
fanning him, sliding
doses of water
down his
throat
slowly with the syringe,

but as quickly as he would take them,

and doused him with a hose, wetting
head,
neck,
and spine;
wiring in there
scorched and peeling from internal heat
like the copper scavenger's fire.

We released him — wobbling
into the pen with the cows,
to suckle
and heal ...

(O' breast of thy mother, balm on the spirit!)

As we watched him go,
a wave of irony came to my face
like a thunderclap
after the flash:

we saved him, treated
and kept him alive,
to be of value —
to grow and die.

FEED

Feed the lives that feed lives.
— Wendell Berry

Everything in the world

clamours for it.

Explosions of grain
on the feedroom floor,

holes bitten
in walls of
stacked bags,

weanlings
crying in the distance.

It travels by desire through the world.

BLOOD WRITING

In the place of horns

is that crazy writing

that says nothing,

everywhere in red.

Pulsing,

expressing on boards,

fence posts, other calves

standing together,

heads bowed

sprouting

delicate wands of blood,

streaming

until the pressure slackens,

factors of coagulation set in,

and the writing

runs out.

THE DRAGMARK

*Calfbook entry: 1/1/01 Cow #34-97 *Calf born dead, presented backwards, legs down, hard pull.*

I will not speak of the dragmark
except to say
it was made without intent —
a phrase of weight against
the ground.

No message of life, not
the tenured beating
of hooves answering
suddenfound power
in delight of the world,

but thing neither
living nor dead, neverborn
or shifted perhaps,
from whisper
to whisper.

Hauled too late into this world
like a soul from beneath a house
collapsed, the grimaced dream of life
frozen in a face that
never saw

winter morning light, moon-
hung mists of autumn
sodden days and fair, none
but this day unseen
upon ground unfelt,

the long, solemn
line of its mass
carved dully all the way
to the place it finally is
and never was.

CHAOS

Has no parent form.

Not the couplet of

calf that won't suck,
cow with swollen,
ground-dragging
udder,

huge, impossible
teats.

Nor a squealing,
snake-caught frog,

or bull which having just broken
the other bull's leg, spends his time
triumphantly taunting, indomitably
screwing him.

If you would live,
love this which passeth all understanding.

If you would love, learn
the hideous power of life.

ARITHMETIC

All dressed in dew,

the earthbound butterfly

is two!

Two sound like ten,

calves alone

in a pen.

Eleventh day of rain,

only mud

is getting fat.

A HORSE DIES BENEATH YOU

for Johnathan Treadway

It's like getting your bearings in an earthquake.

His last step taken and the descent begins,
brick by brick — the horseflesh building you're atop
implodes, crumbles to the
ground,

the lifelong contract
between gravity
and will
breached for good,

and you're caught between horse and earth.

He doesn't understand
why his breaths don't serve him,
head flailing, nostrils flaring like nets
in the white summer air.

You pull your leg free, crawl to your feet,
as he tries to rise, pawing aimlessly.
You step close, undo
the saddle,

lift the bridle
over his ears, loose
the bit, and lastly,
look into his eyes,

that little world
in disarray,

soul
busy packing,

scrambling like a rat
in the feedroom.
Then unbinding itself
like a cough from the chest —

gone.

I have dragged him,
"Top Kick Dude,"
with tractor, buggy, and chain to the place
I took my other horse, "Red Fox."
I rode him 28 years,
beginning when I was ten
and he was two.

I stumble over bones in the grass
to undo the buggy.
It has been seven years
since I brought him here,
a bout of colic, rain, and cold
his undoing, as such a combination
was needed to unlock his life from the world.

A third —
the horse between, "Joker,"
smooth, eloquent gaits,
set beneath a mind in torment.
Heaven never sent a soul to earth

that struggled more and, becoming rabid,
ended in disgrace,

caught in a cattle chute,

euthanized,
dragged just outside the pens where we
decapitated him,
scalped and opened
his skull with a Skil saw,
excised his pink, noodled brain
and turned it over, iced in a cooler
to Animal Control.

We buried him —
head, body, bridle, and tack,
bloodied cloths and blood-stained earth
in a huge hole,
dug with a machine
where he laid, and covered over
like a hideous secret.

Epilogue

I circle the trees,
face him east with the tractor,
loose the chain,
rehook the buggy,
load the saddle and tack,
and head into
the morning glare.

SALE DAY

The breeze
arrives at noon,
with the brightness of day,
Absence is evidence of what's been done
or the warm pool of air that keeps the place they stood,
as we counted and drove them
in scalebox loads to be weighed.

And strange patterns on the road, tire prints
where he backed each time, and
the rash of manure, shaken through
floorboards
of Mickey's trailer when they jumped
through the gates onto the ramp as across a great chasm,
climbing
in single file
hurrying, filling compartments
of the semi trailer like a gigantic
steel bowel hungry for them.

Through hazy morning, we worked,
hustling herds to the pens, parting
cows from calves, sending them ahead
as the "extract" was diverted — calves
door to door, filling crowding pen
and alleyway, moving continuously through the chute, save those
that balked and turned, twisting into knots the crew had to undo
before they flowed again.

Each moment, a number-tagged ear in my hand
"139," I shout above the din.
Old boss's eyes in mine as he leans, cringes as if to hear,
as if I'm about to throw water on him.

"139!" men standing next to him yell.
He hunts the number through pages of prepared lists,
finds and checks it with his pencil —
"Give her to Jack."
Gates switch, chute opens, and calves move again.
another ear in hand (my glasses fogging in the damp heat),
another; steers to the bottom lot, sale heifers in the top, keepers
back with the cows, until we run out of them.

The deal figures in longhand at the scales
on a yellow tablet, weights taken load by load.
three-percent shrink (*our share of calf nobody gets, calf*
that goes up in smoke between here and Oklahoma)
is penciled and subtracted
at the end.

Jack runs the figures on his hand computer,
adding each to an invoice as they weigh.
Old Boss slides the cast metal weight
along a numbered beam rising and falling,
taps it to rest in the middle, looks up each time asking,
"That suit you?"

Jack nods without a word.

Gates throw open
in explosion of hooves,
all of us yelling, slapping, prodding every angle
as the scalebox empties calf by calf,
as if on this day we can do but one thing
and we do it till they're gone.

Noise drains from the yard with the last load.
They sit in the idling truck,
Boss and Jack
in the air conditioning
figuring the check.
Semi on the road full, departing.

Mickey pulls away from the loading ramp
inclined to empty space.
The crew begins loosing the winch to
lower the ramp, lever and undo the wheels (raised
through the loading like a bird's feet in flight),
remounting a side at a time (*one man slides keeper-*
pins into slots, as others pry and hold
each wheel in place).
Put together, the ramp is hooked to a truck,
towed across the bridge, and set off
in the yard.

Old Boss leaves to write paychecks.
We head to the pens to run the cutbacks through the chute,
sort them by herd matching numbers from the list.
Westside calves go down the lane (they take off like rabbits).
We drive the others across the bridge and through the gate
where they disappear into a clutch of young cows.

Around the big table at Mrs. B's
we listen to Mickey's Korean war stories.

(*Fuck orders, it's every man for himself!* he told his
superiors behind enemy lines.)
Tales follow of dayworking on the Kissimmee River,
tending *Mr. Joe Henry's cattle,*
digging a big cypress tree fifty years ago from
Fisheating Creek with a dragline
for old Tom Gaskins at his Cypress Knee Museum.
We listen, eat, drink, and relax
as the calves fly faster than they've ever gone
through worlds they've never seen.

Will they stop between here and Oklahoma? Rob asks Mickey.

Jack has hay and water lined up for them in Alabama.
They'll get there 'round midnight.

At dusk
we let twenty first-calf heifers cross the bridge
and shut them in the pens.
They'll be safe here through tonight.
I tell my son.

I check them at midnight,
a hundred eyes in the headlight swing between
boards of the corral, fixed like stars in the void.
Voices rise like a wind, scaling peaks of sadness
as though none of it can be borne and must come out,
all of them calling, crying against
the silent dark.

DOMESTICITY

POSTHOLE DIGGER'S DREAM

He knew something
inside her

like the softness

deep
in the ground

at the bottom
of
postholes.

What he knew kept him working
when the digging got bad.

THIS MORNING

The last Sunday of the year
in the church hour,
while the children are away, cattle fed,
and chickens turned out in the yard,

we fill the woodbox of the stove,
shut off the lights,
close all the doors of the house,
and let ourselves back into Eden.

How fair are its gates!
How lovely the foilage and warm the light
and you — my one companion
and soul's delight.

DOMESTICITY

Slowly,

with certain regularity,

we get done what we ought.

Eventually

(after three litters of multi-colored kittens),

we spay the cat,

repair the door,

change burnt-out bulbs,

divide the children's room,

buy new tires for the car,

and somehow pay the bills,

keeping apace of our domesticity —

a step ahead of the banker,

a moment behind convention,

putting off heaven and hell

as long as possible.

BURIAL OF THE FREEZER ITEMS

Brought together on the drainfield mound, items
evicted from a crowded freezer by an irate spouse.
Things intended as painting subjects, objects
to study and draw, inedible possibility
en masse, committed to common grave,
after months (if not years)
of suspended animation,
to include *A la Carte:*

birds,
fish,
a snake
and other creatures,
cuts of meat, organs and parts,
things that would nowise
come together, save in this entree
carried to a final resting place, served
unto nature (albeit *the dust),* that something about this
might be settled.

The Main Course:
young purple gallinule
wrapped in plastic that the cold wouldn't spoil
his foilage (pale yellow-green, webbed feet
folded beneath his violet cloak).
Fallen squirrel from the yard, tail wrapped like a shawl
around him, sheathed in a corrugated, cardboard mailer
as though he'd been posted to this waiting room of the
underworld.

Tiny bird, found on the road
where he'd been hit,
the approximate size and weight
of a colored Christmas bulb,
wrapped in foil, and stowed
in a pocket of the freezer door
with boxes of frozen peas
and an icy dish of grease.
Mole the cat dragged in,
barefooted dirt diver dressed
in black velvet.
Coral snake —
half crushed, marinated
in the remaining poison-mingled moisture
of an uncapped soda bottle; left without word
on the doorstep by a friend.

Four sets of long black horns
in a green foam produce tray,
cut from the calves last April.
One steer became infected and swollen,
docked from the load on sale day
by the cowbuyer, fed with the replacement heifers
till he healed, as a solution to his untimely presence.

Calve's testicles
from late winter work, porcelain like
shapes toled in ice and decorated
in fine lavender squiggles, strange artifice
commended to earth as their former hosts graze
somewhere in the grasslands of Oklahoma,
unaware of what precedes them
to the nether realm.

Other parts from the grocer's case,
chicken feet — tree roots they suggest
or fruit-picker's hands, truncated
by seven year's abysmal prices,
kept in lament for lost family land: the "home grove,"
eighty acres of citrus sold for development —
pushed into windrows, piled, and burned.

Last thing, a beef heart —
set among livers, kidneys, and tripe —
the largest, most decorous one chosen
in homage to my father awaiting bypass surgery.
Glistening seams and rivulets incised upon striations of muscle,
like canals cut through strata of rock, gardens of fat
cultivated to excess along its bloodcourses
and cap.

In the hole they go,
joining remains of lost pets,
gravel of drain routes,
bits of brick, terra cotta, glass,
and other uncovered
homestead effects.

What does it mean
for these things
to pass through
hands
and doors
on their way through life?

Taken
to be held,

imagined, consumed, or
in the end, neglected and cast
from
distracted life

to the ground.

To someday arise …
atom by
atom,
piece by piece,
recombining life's myriad
ingredients

at the pace mountains
are made, lifting,
climbing
the worm's
ladder,
to return
to the collection
of ideas
called
the world.

STATE OF LOVE

It is simple to say I love you.

Morning wakens us
shed of animosity,
weathers of anger dissipated,
passing like a front
in the night.

Now we're entwined,
your face I kiss
and cherish, everything
dividing us somehow
slept or worn away
through the dark.

We've returned to the elemental
state of love,
something between us
neither asked for
or known
until it fell into our hands.

ODE TO THE WORKSHIRTS

Finally he wore out the workshirts

taken from the rack

of what used to go to town

on his or his father's back.

More hole than shirt, these

old plaid skins missing

buttons, pockets, sleeves,

windows in their walls

where windows shouldn't be.

Writ upon in the mud's scumbling

insignia, the engine's oily

calligraphy, painted,

spattered, glued, discarded —

never again to catch the stains of being,

of pleasure, labor, wrongdoing.

What they wiped from life and carried,

wash-hamper to waste-bin

they strangely inhabit,

remnant of the earthbound

not yet taken flight.

THE DOANE COLLEGE CHOIR GIRLS

The smell of the Doane College choir girls
lingers in the house.

Damp remains in their towels
gathered from the bathroom,
and imprints not yet

smoothed by my wife's hands
from the spread and pillows
where they slept.

Scents of morning toiletries and immense suitcases
fill the car on the run back to church,
through fog and small talk of Nebraska.

That smell!
Odor of the distant horizon.

BY WHICH SIN?

By which sin did she perish,

hen
of golden feathers,
decapitated, and hanging
in the fence, just outside the pen
this morning?

Distraction (if it's a sin).

The long occasion of dinner into
dark, lengthy phone call afterward.
And mis-remembrance before bed
as the creature came calling for her,
crossing the unlocked, overkept
threshold.

Later
a half-dreamt query —
Did you shut the chicken door?
passed between us,
fading into
sleep.

Sloth.

Unmended
overtrusted holes
in the fabric of the coop.
Faulty seams in its ceiling
unbound and rusting, unnailed corners
of the little plywood house, made

in shortage of cash, energy, and good sense,
built on spousal insistence,
at workweek's end; weakness
and fatigue prefabricated into
domesticity's early chore —
by this was she undone?

Or negligence.

Mounding manure, mouldering hay,
stale water in the bucket or diseased
in a fallow pool of the backyard
by the broken septic line where
she drank. Perhaps she was dead

where he found her, or groggy?
Broody hens unbanished from the laying boxes,
warming inanimate ungathered eggs,
all the safe places full, keeping her out, at risk
in this business that isn't a business.

Misgiving perhaps.

Hens of diminishing number, too smart
to put themselves to bed seeing what
happens inside
when things go awry,
they have to be found after dark, roused from perches
in the trees, coaxed onto a pole and
lowered

to the ground,
chased into the pen before closing the door
until after a week of nights,
we tire of this and another
disappears by morning
light.

Lust, Greed.

The double-roostered threat,
let out each morning, hens
cornered by them as they take turns,
raw necks and bare-backs
evidence

of brutality.
And cowards they,
keeping high in the rafters
when danger comes knocking
upon the
lowly.

Survival, sin of life.

Our every morsel taken,
breath drawn, accursed wish —
no less than his, calling
her demise, the
exchange

between what destroys
and saves. Which sin of these,
I wonder as I close the hole in the ground,
turn without whisper
of prayer,

save —

the rest of this day,
we all be well.

AFTER LOVE,

I peer into
your watery gaze,
pool of reflection
in my eyes.

We laugh at each other
uncontrollably;
how serious we were
moments ago,

rapt
in pleasure's pain —
flung into gyrations of sex
like children trapped on a merry-go-round.

It is laughable we're naked,
stacked on one another
like plastic toy animals
designed to be so.

Caught
in this act we ritually perform,
waging our own little war
against our death.

VISION

METAMORPHOSIS

Then one day

you put the tractor in gear,

rev the engine

and drive straight into the gate.

Watch the fury of splinters flying,

feel the latch and hinges breaking,

find yourself in a place

you've never been before —

the golden flesh of the wood,

and a little of your unfathomable will,

suddenly visible.

POEM OF DEVICE

A Lament

The trees across the way are gone
and with them summer's green
alacrity, lush golden
lampshades of spring.

No more spoonfuls of leaves
set on the rim of heaven, but
tineless forks probing
steep swaths of sky.

Now banished with the shade,
noises of a road once hidden:
equipment, transports, and busses
of fruit pickers towing

rattling trailers of ladders,
come to gather the eternal
math of the land.

Trees are gone from sight,
canopies vanished
in fresh graves of light.

VISION

How do we come to see what we see?
The goldfish caught against the intake
pipe of the aquarium filter
where he struggled for hours unseen,
calf slow to rise at the far end of the field,
sticks like a warped penny in a slot of your mind
as the herd drains through the gate
into fresh pasture.

And things that are nothing:

dark animal shapes on fencelines
between tree-hem and ground
don't bear out as you approach,
or light passing through trees,
illuminating in a sudden flare,
some ordinary thing,
drawing you halfway across a tract
to see what has always been.

But the heifer
with her head caught between
tree trunks goes unnoticed until
the day you enter the woods, find
her withered shadow, throw of hide
over skull, bones and scraps — artifact
of something realized and at the same instance,
lost.

Oh mind, concept, days …
Bring me not again to another
of these moments!

One morning
you turn in the room,
catch a mirrored figure in the hall,
bespectacled, grizzled,
older and heavier
than you'd suppose.
A stranger before you,
known all along.

WINTER

As if color
had been banished
from elsewhere, these
birds appear

replacing leaves
of trees,
disquieting
silence.

A painted bunting at the feeder
with his chartreuse wife,
others in scarlet, indigo
and tinier birds, Christmas-bulb sized

in pale yellow and blue.
They cross half a continent
to be here, audacity
askance of the season's

austerity
yet another kind of proof.
Cedar waxwings —
a sudden forty

quivering in a treetop —
give the chilly wind
a figure before disappearing
in a breath,

gone
as if they were never here,
like all souls lost
from this day.

COMMUNION

Flashes dance the ceiling
over silver trays filled
with white cubes, passing
through the pews.

My face askew
on the rim of
this momentary
mirror as I take
a piece and
hand it on.

Bread

squishes between my
fingers in and out of square
into an oblong ball,

and we wait.

As we wait,

light glimmers on the lake.
The cola-colored universe beneath
our dock is home to several
tiny planets on hooks.

Doughball waterworld real estate
of the adolescent fishing pole gods
under seige of minnows,
hundreds —

This is the body of Christ, broken for you,
Take and eat . . .

Rustle of hands rising,
penetrance of taste,
saliva and prayer.

Home at noon,
children spill from the car
chasing about the yard in Sunday clothes.

Sharon opens the coop pouring Jesus
leftovers from a plastic bag into a clutch of hens
that peck and scratch

and strew the soft remains
of the Lord into this world
of the sacramental hunger.

SUMMER HEART

for Lawrence Hetrick

I'll wait all summer, as I have,
to feel August's air cross the room
rendering ceiling-fans silly, catch the children
colds and begin the glacial return of the covers
to the pillows.

I will wait as I have for the pink of
dawn when the autumn stars rise, barely
to be seen, yet certain, as the bill
follows the meterman,
in the sky.

Something I didn't mention —
the lonely planet of the morning
suffering summer's end (I know he is lonely and suffers
for the singing he does to himself),

not him,
the thing like him
I'll await as a rock
the river flows past,
this eighth month of the year.

YOUR LIFE, YOUR DEATH

The shoes you put on your feet this morning
another man may take off tonight.
— anon

This is your life,
your storehouse of things —
the dust, dirt, and mildew
your life attracts, on surfaces of the idle things
of your life.

Here are shelves filled
with tools, parts, books,
necessary things arranged
as only you would have them,
and things that no longer matter — broken,
unused or forgotten things.
Here are cans of leftover paint, jars of varnish, and glue
with rusted seals and frozen lids.
Bottles of mordant, acid, and ground are where they were last used,
coated in the fine powder of time.

A half-opened vice on the bench
is littered with filings now rusted, an anvil
rests on the floor, askance, and bench grinder inhabits
a corner of the room on its homemade stand.

Power tools
with rolled up
cords fill the steps
to the loft among other tools:

wrenches,
screwdrivers,

hammers, chisels, and bits,
blades, belts, fasteners,
plane, square, chalk-box,
and tinsnips, goggles,
nailpouch, apron, smock,
and what is either stored beneath
or fallen behind
the stairs over time.

All such things are present
that follow the context of your life.

In the open spaces of the room, unfinished
paintings line the walls in plain view.
Some have stood for months, seasons, years;
others were begun last week.

Taboret and palette, easel, and stool,
paintbox full of pigments,
and bucket of brushes soaking in spirits
overlook the corner stilllife table set
with a musty cloth — chalk and charcoal
markings on its surface, circumscribe missing
things — vessels, crusts of fruit, an imploded squash (seeds
adrift in the ruined flesh), desiccated vines, stems, and curled,
fallen leaves amid roach and mouse droppings and egg-cases
of drosophila, accompanying stains of blood, rust, oil, and other
remainders from which a painting has taken
flight.

Shovels, hoe, pitch-fork, axe and pick, and fresh-cut staves lean
against the open side of the table.

Bevy of skulls:
horse, pig, cow,
and human, with
jawbones,
scapulae,
vertebrae,
and turtle shells
stow in the shadows beneath
the table in common suspense.

Empty frames dangle
from the joists of the loft among various
hand saws hooked on nails by their handles.
Lengths of chain,
a pail of obstetrical tools, can
of saddle-grease,
load-binder and pulleys,
lantern, longshoreman's grapple,
steel traps, and sprig of dried bay leaves, strung
by its binding — hang
interspersed between three naked bulbs
illuminating sectors of the room.

Drawings,
prints, and leaves of paper
comingle in heaps on the draughting table and floor,
and fill drawers of the flatfile,
in unmitigated chronology, evidence old and new
of the limits of an imagination.

This is your life —
house that contains it,
place you spend your days,

where everything will be
when you stop,
your hands and feet stayed
and heart quiets in its chamber for good.

Outside,
backed into place against
the small porch, a tractor and buggy,
legs and packmule of your existence.

On its deck:
buckets of staples and nails,
fence-tools and stretcher,
gloves, bale of new wire
(and rusty hoops of old), shovel,
posthole digger, posts,
pruning saw,
and machete,
lariat, jug of water, and
blocks of wood.

Across the way, at the entrance to the yard,
the angle, incline, and width of the crossing,
all determined so long ago, and dangers
affixed to your life by design,
belong to you as do puddle holes in the driveway
that keep their places (despite everything).

The edge and fact of the road, its grade
tended weekly by the county machine,
and ingredients —
blonde sands, silver fines, brittles
of rock and lime, fragments

of bone and shells (their bright, bleached
otherness you've wondered about your whole life),
insect carapaces, trails of slugs and worms,
and lines of ants hauling burdens from source
to burrow in constant streams upon this scrim.

Things of season: the autumn mast,
pollens of spring,
whole limbs felled in summer afternoon storms,
litter of fronds, sticks, and leaves,
the shadows of trees,
interrupting
that brightness along its length
out to the edges of your life.
The entire particularity of your existence —

flowing above,
beneath and around you,
where you go, and what you do,
in each day's passing,
laying treads of your machines,
prints of your feet, turning
as a giant ball, receiving
you every moment
it throws you at the world,

stopping
as you stop,
waiting
while you eat and rest,
moving again when you're
ready to roll.
This is your life

which, as far as you know,
goes on forever.

This is how death comes:

arriving unseen,
wearing your clothes,
tying your shoes, appearing
in the mirror — something
you can't recognize, but know full and well.
A false sense, misgiven notion,
mistaken assurance, wrongful
assumption.

The dog you beat, horse
you let run, gate
you don't open
or forget to shut,
letting weeds grow,
fences go, misjudged weather,
rotted leather, overhanging
limb,

dangling vine, loosened nuts,
hidden hole, unravelled twine.
the pipe you don't clear
when it's dry, or can't
when it rains, unhoned
knife, missing chain,
dulled saw, wrung threads,
ungreased fitting, climb

you haven't strength
to take, difference
a year makes.
Forging ahead,
quitting too soon,
anger, tiredness,
distraction,
greed.

Song of the spinning blades
as you draw near, caress
of the morning breeze,
upon your skin
light —
as you are not a creature of darkness.
The dark and your need for
peace and sequestration.

Present every moment,
rare to the world,
invites you often,
takes you once.
The last thing you know
the first moment

your life
becomes a story.

ALBUM

ELEGY FOR CATHY

Dear Cathy —
The very book in which I write
wouldn't be in my hands but for you.

It was your love that
refined me, led me
to verse and books.
How can I think of your demise
except this way — a death of love.

A death made in love: cancelled
appointments, and prescriptions (what a joy!),
taxes paid, arrangements made,
not the plans of a literary femme fatale
but a farm girl's sensibility, pockets

stuffed with pure Midwestern will,
not the world's charitable quotient of rocks
and no swiftly moving current
but stillness you lay beneath, girl
of Kansas, beloved angelheart.

How many times did you rise back
at the sight of overpassing clouds?
And the cold of the pond where
the dog also took itself to die,
did its wetness not waken you,

test your theory of death
with each failing breath?
How could such a thing be done at all
save by you, daughter of broad skies,
the undersurface of that pool but a lens

opened on certain heaven, coverlet
drawn upon yourself to sleep
before waking in an elsewhere morning,
broken upon chores, newborn calves
and fresh-mown hay.

PARIS SUITE

The way here is exacting,

requires a certain discomfort

and lack of sleep.

On the plane we examine French currency,

bills exchanged for our money

at a bank in Palm Beach

(there is a buying and a selling price).

We hold the notes against the overhead light,

see images of great artists,

composers, architects,

and writers —

Cézanne on money!

Debussy, Eiffel,

Antoine de Saint-Exupéry

(his little prince also).

Sharon sleeps all afternoon

the day of our arrival as I go about town

with a headache, half lost, paying

the French their money

with trepidation. They

know more about it than I.

I am not eager to spend my Cézannes.

INSECT POEM

Angry little ant —

it is your job

to bite me,

mine

to crush you.

KANSAS

June, 1996 from the NCBA Young Cattlemen's tour

One morning, something in your life brings you to Kansas
and, it's six a.m. in the Sunday streets of Garden City
beneath ominous skies.

Smells of the feedyard whip around town
wound in the wind, adding to its vagaries,
a lone soda can driving down the street.

Here are strip malls, real estate offices, and a laundromat
that could be anywhere, only this is Kansas,
and you've never been here before.

Such is middle America — spread upon the continent like a replicating
dream, long ago, claimed
as our own.

Who will shop at Target,
eat at Burger King, and live
in the houses that all look alike?

Who, now grown familiar with the endless tracts of grain along the road,
will live the intersection stories and watch their children
come and go like weather?

Kansas, made upon this ground,
certain as center pivot irrigation,
(the magic circle devoted to agriculture),

cut-down trees (where there were any to cut),
relief of whiskey, much-needed rain, and the sudden happiness

that comes to your face by nearly anything out of the ordinary.

Such is its poem, place
so far from anywhere
it is everywhere.

Simple in a sense:

the green land,
purple sky,
and what comes of this

vast,
unattended
drama of regularity.

America is a man who doesn't understand the ways of his heart,
and Kansas is a place this man calls home.

WOMAN

Life flows from mighty woman,
legs like trees growing from her roots,
defying her own gravity of a kind
space probes report from other planets
(a teaspoonful, the weight of twenty elephants).

Has not the entire race of men fallen from orbit into her?

It is in their faces, a power they wield
that frightens men so, who keep myths
and blunt implements against them,
spaying, veiling and vilifying,
stripping the world of religions they make,

holding God between, though God is a woman.
She alone knows this and tries each moment to tell us,
yet in deceit and fear we go about our ways
ruining things we love and in so doing,

come to understand hell.

Life moves ever forth from woman.

She's survived centuries of imperfect men, outliving

most, taking the balance when she goes.

She was sent to rid the world of its other force

and would do so easily, save at her every footfall

a man springs up.

ALBUM

Ama la vida a la frontala, porque buena o mala, solo tenemos una.
— Anon

In the album, pages of old photographs
of lives gone by — that beautiful past
with its great future still struggling to arrive.
Little did they in the pictures know or forsee us,
not as we can look page by page,
into the sepia softness
and see them:

Early farm in Shelby County, Indiana.
The Sexton clan and family dog posed
for a picture against the broad side of the house.
A tattered, striped cloth spread beneath them
over uneven ground, its pattern
biased against the clapboards
behind.

Sarah and Issac Sexton, seated
and dour, serious as life,
progenitors of all family flesh
and events to follow. Nadir to zenith: from
Bert's depression and demise by his own hand
(and Lucy's 70 years later),
to the raising of a mountain. How sad to know the stories
and behold this world at such remove —
formality of dress, manners, and evidence of
good food, wholesome labor and living,
with ample time for it all.

Proud siblings stand together, young adults,
the eldest with spouses, swaddlings in arms,

children at their feet.
Waldo and Will, couplet of brotherly love
(before Will drowned rescuing victims in a flood).
Moon-faced Rhoda, who "cried and cried" when Waldo left for school,
and sophisticated Lulu who said,
It is a luxury to be understood.
All before lives expanded — Waldo left to see the world,
crossing the country to places, things unimaginable,
arriving in the tropics of undeveloped,
east-coastal Florida.

New pictures in pages far beyond Indiana:
W.E. and Elsebeth Sexton outside their piney homestead
in the shadow of cabbage trees and strangler fig
in full embrace.

Another of Waldo, standing in the garden plot with shovel in hand,
When I met him," she said, *He was living in one room*
and kept the other full of feed.

He,
who wrote his young bride on her trip home to Franklin Park,
Go out and look at the moon, see if it's as bright or as romantic
a moon as a Florida moon and tell me in your reply.
I've forgotten how a northern moon looks.

A page later, he is leaning against backdoor steps,
first child cradled in his arms, his gaze
pouring into her face as if everything to come
could be divined in those eyes.

Other pictures, rooms added to the house —
breakfast-porch, and upper story, the homestead

unrecognizable from its beginnings. And children
on the rise, faces frozen in the early morning of life's full day.
Visages serious and full of pride, vanities of pubescence —
daughters with boyfriends on their minds, little brothers
underfoot (all feet bare), wearing baggy,
boy-filled trousers, riding white ponies
in the front yard.

Manured affluence.
Cane syrup and whiskey-making turned to stands of citrus,
ocean-front lots on the barrier island (only reached by boat
and stretches of imagination).
Farm ventures with out-of-town investors
(Waldo's sweat and Mr. Davis's cash),
grown into real estate deals, a dairy,
products company, and packing house.

A photograph from the upstairs balcony frames
a white prom dress full of daughter set against
the world. A Seminole Indian in another, shooting
a coconut off Barbara's head with bow and arrow.
Jacqueline at the beach with a chimpanzee
on her shoulders. Later, her wedding to Jack,
parents and betrothed, best man and maid of honor,
together on the lawn in white suits, the splendid
tropical antiquity of wild, unfathomed Indian
River County (before its designation)
pressing in at every edge.

Florida:
the land,
her children,
essence and mystery —

there for the taking
by any and all,
present or passing through.

Pinky is here from Arizona.
He's been coming all week by bus
to court Barbara, but she'd rather have John
just back from Europe, war hero, football player, Texan.
Pinky returns to Arizona, dejected.

Jack and Jackie are called to parishes up north,
then around Florida, finally to California,
building family and church on the other side of the "world."

Barbara and John marry, buy the dairy,
build a house next door; children are born.
A whole generation arrives, we:
little ones they used to be, cousins
gathered together on weekends, holidays,
to work out the terms of relationship,
an occasion at a time.

A family Christmas photograph gathers us around
103-year-old Grandma Martens in her chair, great-grandmother
of all mankind, monument of bone and blood.
Her flesh withering as we flourish, grandchildren
in front, parents young and beautiful, behind,
not even half the mistakes of their lives yet made.

It is the complete moment of family, everyone,
alive, together in place.

Now the pictures come in color.

Elsebeth's wake: the family gathered
outside Randy's house beneath a backyard gazebo
Waldo and Grandma Martens long ago passed;
other faces are gone from the crowd.
Jackie is missing Jack. John is missing the lower third
of his descending colon. Barbara has Parkinson's.
both boys divorced.

All the cousins are grown and married. Some moved away
as young families, arise in new waves of children
brought together on Christmas, Easter, Thanksgiving,
and the Fourth of July consequence
of family.

We spend lives we haven't time to live,
full of memories, knowledge, joys and fear
our children barely comprehend.
A former world has retreated into
the album.

Even now we perceive our own disappearance,
a fading against new morning light.

In Memoriam: John Ellis Daley, John Robert Tripson,
Barbara Louise Tripson, and Charles Randolph Sexton.

TO THE ORGAN

... then the Lord God formed man of dust from the ground and breathed into his nostrils the breath of life, and man became a living being. — Gen.2: 7

I

To speak this thing,
begin with the fundament:

A
man
returns
from war,
property
disputes
settled,
pursuit
of
lovely
faces
ended,
blood
and
dark
-ness
but
three
steps
back
from
certain
dawn.

Peace,
order,
indus
-try
(and
hope)

w
i
t
h
in
grasp;
music
arises
in him
inevit-
able
as
spring
flowers,
grows
like a
joyous
wind
he
sends
into
empty
hollow
things

as
God
gives
breath
to
empty
hollow
man,
cause-
ing all
such
things
to
sing!

II

A principality,

place
between
heaven and earth,
full of what might be
and what has always been —

country of the organ.

Orchestra
in all its motion,
and breath.

You,
inside this
dwelling place of effects,

as in a guitar, between
wood-paneled walls
and string-crossed
hole to the sky,

or recumbent in the bell of a horn,
upon a couch of air,
the furniture of this parlor
aloft, voices

of bands, instruments,
and chorus,

a body of sound
inside its birthplace, always

inside, as
a river in its banks

running eternally
from its source
until overflowing,
washing everything away.

Country of the organ,
place between heaven and earth.

III

The stops.
Separations of pressure
into districts of sound:

Principal
Flutes
Strings
Reeds.

Ranks of pipes fed from the great cabinet of wind
like boroughs of a city built by the sea
with aerodynamic streets and alleyways,
an economy founded on air.

The inevitable division of labor:

Swell,
Positiv,
Haptwerk,
Choir.

Grand households and families of this city,
their good names:

Aeoline, Amorosa,
Apfelrugal,
Bauerflote,
Basoonell,
Bombardon,
Como d' Amore,
Cremena, and *Cuckoo.*

Lineages
of the country of the organ
each of a craft and trade,
derivations of shape

and sound, different
as the species
of glasses
of a well-stocked bar.

Flutings,
stems and hollows,
bells, volume, and depth,
each different and

distinct
to its purpose,
servile to a task.
Vases,

ever poured into and out of
with decants of wind,
washed with emptiness
to be filled again.

And the tastes and variety
of its stock in trade:
liqueurs and aperitifs, clear strains
and whiskies,

ales, lagers, and stouts,
juices and carbonates,

wines of distinction
and common fare.

All specialties of the house.
That is the
organ.

Its folk —

singing, crying
in happiness,
pleasure, travail,
and woe.

Voices:

Gamba,
Glockenspeil and *Gongs,*
Marimba,
Melophone,
Musette,
Nachthorn,
Ocarina and *Oboe,*
Philomela and *Piffaro.*

Flora of breath
in the great varietal botany of music.

Sackbut,
Scharfregal,
Sesquialtera, Stenthorn,
Terzzimbel,
Tibia Dura,

Tromboncini,
Tuba Sonora,

members
of an extraordinary society,
aggregations of kind.

Unda Maris,
Viola Pomposa,
Vox Humana,
Zymbalscharf —

Birdful of feathers,
headful of hairs,
uncountable digits
of gigantic hands and feet,
bristling whistles
of copper and nickel
set in little beds with
great delicacy and taste,
planted beneath hedges of pipes,
horns sprouting everywhere,
row upon row.

All this as though planned
and brought into being at the edge
of a wood, near the feet of great
and veritable trees!

Pedal pipes —
ten-, twenty-foot boxes
of oak and ash

stood on end
soughing,
murmuring
like old growth forest
in an afternoon breeze.

Planted in shade,
rooted in air,
an entire garden
has risen to stand

in darkness.

IV

Yet this is no garden, orchard,
or wood,

but a man,
trapped in a wall,
with his thoughts, singing
to himself.

Like any life,
what you see is the small part —
the cordial, made-up face,
shiny, expectant mouth,
eyes open, orifices agape,
and beneath the surface
of this like-sum of being
are things tied together
in the dark, structures
knit and glued, long reaches
of bone crossed and joined,
innumerable connections,
articulations:

finger to heart,
toe to mind,
bowel to eye,
ear to foot.

And all of it hitched

to lungs
innnermost,

eternally pulsing,
heart driven tides of air.
An indoor tornado, calamitous
and coursing through channels,
vessels, capillaries and valves,

filling, emptying and
filling again, pressurizing every
part, vitals and extremities,
bottom to top, inside-
out with the tonus
and rigour of
its life.

All taking place
invisibly to you
but just like you —

a body of parts
bearing hunger, want
and need, its burden
of dreams, hope, and
despair,
all set in motion
with each inhalation.

Machine alas,
beneath it all,
with valves, pistons,
pinions and gears,
springs,
catches,
louvers

and stays.

Opening,
closing,
spinning,
turning,
running interminably
at the service of quiet,
constant respiration:

breath awaiting touch.

V

Not one man but many
make up this thing,
draughtsman and engineer,
designer and salesman,
an army of tradesmen
at the bottom
of this grand concoction:

plumber, electrician,
cooper and welder,
carpenter, cabinetmaker,
computer expert and smith —
jacks of all trades and those,
solitary and frustrated, who travel
about, voicing these structures
of sound.

The player,

half an octoped —
arms and legs
in motion,
ten fingers,
two feet
working, bringing
everything to the surface,
throwing switches, turning keys,
checking mirrors, programming,
strategizing, piloting
to far away ports of call,
spending his life aboard ship —

passing hours, weeks, seasons,
time of no accounting, studying,
learning, hoping, regretting.

Overwhelmed
is he at the helm or overboard,
drowning
in an ocean of effects,
lost in a forest, caught in foul weather,
driving all night through the fog.

Mouse in man's greatest trap.

Reaching, grasping,
prodding,
poking,
slapping, stabbing,
diminishing,
soaking,

combing cobwebs of melody in fingersful,
tossing tremulous bales by the shoulderload,
the soft caressing of chins,
hard taken hammer strokes on shins,
yanking cloths from beneath dishes,
chunking bricks through window glasses.

evoking,
ringing,
saying,
singing,

mourning, weeping,

shouting, bleating,
imitating earthquakes,
insects,
and beasts,

strings wailing,
horns blowing,

a bottomless basso profundo,
the noon whistle's human crescendo.

Each,
a manual and stops

which is to say —
fingers and thoughts,

which is to say —
scheme, rehearsed, or impromptu

which is to say —
matter of theory, labor, and intent

which is to say —
hope, vanity, and history, bound
in every touch, and not just touch but weaving,
culturing what comes forth.

Pulling knobs, rolling dials,
treading pedals,
hopping keys,

imposing,
engaging,
employing,
arranging

all its elements as one might plan
a sumptuous feast,
setting the menu:
soup,
appetizers,
salad and bread,
main course and dessert,
from a chef who cuts
and dices with
every move.

Spicemaster,
saucesmith,
abattoir, and
grocer
filling and emptying
pantries for his audience.

Provider and plunderer,
steward and vandal,
gatekeeper, wrestler,
freemason, thief,

pugilist,
gymnast,
doctor,
magician,
stevedore,

mesomorph,
monk,
and athlete,

Ox in its traces, alone and tired,
mule of burden,
yet kingly and inspired,
proprietor, servant,

mayor, and lowliest denizen
of this place between heaven and earth.

VI

Who can know his last hour?

Who can choose the final moment
you find yourself
wending along a dark course
between elsewheres,
brambles of light
ahead.

Who can say
when strange hands
will come to you, untie
and take off your shoes,
unfamiliar fingers tend and coiff
and dress you for a Sunday
that lasts forever?

And you arrive in a grand parlor,
country of the organ —
place between heaven
and earth, flowers,
friends, and
remaindermen
filling aisles and pews,

hands astir,
hearts and faces
fluttering, moistened in
weathers of tears.
You —
like music

around the room,

in the country of the organ,
between heaven
and earth. You,
like sound on the walls,
in the ceiling ever arriving and escaping
into air from chimneys of the houses
of the country of the organ,

between heaven and earth.
Sadness and joy,
darkness, light,
forethought and retrospect,
all together combusting
into music in the country
of the organ.

Heaven.
Earth.
You —
the far-flung song
of a pipe at the core
of your being

in the country
of the organ,
heaven and
earth.

You,
at last
like music.

THE WORLD

One thing at a time
is what the world says,

as I get up for more grits, propping
pages with honey-jar and spoon,

and the book slips, flings itself
shut.

LIST OF ILLUSTRATIONS

AFTERWORDS

Quote accompanying "Album," page 93, as found posted in a small seaside restaurant in Playa del Carmen during a trip to the Yucatan Peninsula in 1995 is taken to mean: *Love your life and face it, because good or bad, we only have one.*

"To the Organ" was largely conceived and written over several years, during American Guild of Organists concerts in churches around Vero Beach and practice sessions of Jose Daniel Flores in the Community Church sanctuary, Vero Beach, FL.

Thanks to Lawrence Hetrick for initial and subsequent edits of the poems and much advice, as well as to Mike and Marilyn Kemp, Patrick Smith, Deborah Worsfold, Lowry Smathers and Lauris London whose readings, encouragements, and belief in this volume have kept it (and me) afloat. Thanks as well to Steve Bradbury whose suggestions about poems and pictures helped to configure this volume inside and out into its present state. I have a special angel, Carissa Neff, who has given immeasurably to both manuscript and author in her reading and comments in the perfect hour. A special mention of two dear friends who infected me with a love for poetry early on, Cathy Turner and Hali Denton.

Thanks as well to the inestimable Rick Campbell and his organization that shines pure light into a world bereft of poetry (becoming more so each day) and Lynne Knight, booksmith, confidant, and magician.

And of course, my great wife!

ABOUT THE AUTHOR

Sean Sexton was born in Indian River County and grew up on his family's Treasure Hammock Ranch, eight miles west of Vero Beach, Florida. He divides his time between taking care of a 600-acre cow-calf and seed-stock operation and painting and writing. He is married to artist Sharon Sexton, and they live on the ranch with their two children in a house they built with their hands.

He has kept journal-sketch books drawn from his life since 1973 and was awarded an Individual Artist's Fellowship from the State of Florida in 2000-2001. He is the author of *Waldo's Mountain, Brief History of a Small Elevation* (Waterview Press, 2001) about his grandfather, Waldo Sexton.